I Am Cissy

Journey of the Millionaire Woman

Overcoming Mistakes and the Real Deal About Being a Successful Black Female Entrepreneur

CISSY WATKINS

1/1/21

Printed in the United States of America

First Printing, 2020

ISBN 978-0-578-79960-5

www.IAmCissy.com

Table of Contents

Whatever purpose God has put in your heart,
IT IS FOR YOU! Never Give Up. Enjoy.
Have Fun. Live. Love. Laugh. Learn. And Serve.
Great Blessings Over Your Life Always.

-Cissy Watkins

Dedication

This book is dedicated to my three children—Alex, Taylar, and Leslie. You are the manifestation of the legacy that God entrusted to me. You guys are my life and have been there with me every step of the way. I am so proud of the young women and the man that you have become. Equipping you for successful lives has been the joy of my life.

I am so blessed to be your mother!

Many people do not know the origin story of the name of my cleaning company. Look no further than this part of the dedication. A(lex), T(aylar), L(eslie), and C(issy) are the reason for the name ATL&C Cleaning Service. What a great way to keep the main goal of creating a successful legacy for my family in front of me at all times!

Alex my Prince, Taylar my Sunshine, and Leslie my Princess—

I Love You to Life!

Special Dedications

To my father, Lewis Henry Watkins (LH). You are my hero and I am so grateful to have you. Your guidance, inspiration, and unyielding courage have set the markers for me and fueled the desire for me to create a legacy that is Kingdom based and successful.

I can never thank you enough for the foundation that you helped to build in me—self-confidence, perseverance, determination, focus, and faith, among other things. Thank you for your wisdom and all the kitchen table talks. I love you!

To my beloved mother, Hattie Watkins. I Am because of you. I watched you over countless years, taking care of people, giving out so much, and very rarely receiving anything in return. I used to wonder if you expected to receive anything from people that you served with a relentless heart. I witnessed what my future could look like by watching how you lived and the lessons that you taught me.

I remember showing you my 2020 vision at the kitchen table, and you told me you were proud of me. You told me the more successful you get, people will only see you for what you can give and do. They will forget that you are human also. I asked you what you meant about forgetting that I am human. You said that they won't see your pain, your sad days, your struggles; they only want what you can give and do. You told me to never forget about me in this journey (it was like you already knew that I had) and to always do what I wanted to do. Thank you for supporting me in all my ups and downs in this journey called life. I Am Cissy because God choose you to be my mother!

I love you, Mommy. Rest in Heaven Forever my Lil Girl.

To my Auntie Tommie McConnell – Thank you for always keeping my eyes and heart focused on God's Word and for being transparent. You have kept it 100 with me and given me the listening ear that I needed whenever I needed it. Thank you!

To my forever best friend Gina Crawley-Anderson – We have been friends for 35 years. Even though we have spent time apart, we never missed a beat! Our rhythm is God's Divine order. No matter what life has thrown my way, you have never let go of my hand, and that has meant the world to me. I look forward to this new journey with you. I also look forward to sitting in the backyard (yes outside lol) and growing old together! I Love you, My Sister!

To My Confidante – You keep me rooted and grounded, encouraging me to live free and to be my authentic self and to live with no regrets.

You have been my safe haven when I am with you giving me strength in spirit to move forward in my life. You are a take charge individual who keeps me full of joy and happiness. You connect with me on an intimate level and you know how to handle my needs and my wants all at the same time. I cannot put a value on what you have been to me. What you have brought to my life is just as priceless as you are.

I Love you. #Leftie

To My Family, Friends, Loved Ones, Business Partners, and Colleagues – You have played, and continue to play, an important role in my journey to success. I appreciate each one of you and I look forward to the chance to continue to love you, support you, and build with you far into the future. I am grateful for you.

Foreward

My name is Jai Staton. I am a mother, an entrepreneur, a writer, and a business professional. I met The Millionaire Woman, Cissy Watkins, over 10 years ago through a business referral from a mutual friend. Our relationship has grown into a trusted sisterhood since then.

I am overjoyed to introduce you to Cissy, my sister, best friend, colleague, and mentor.

Cissy is a woman of God who has been relentless in her faith and resilient in her purpose. She shares the love of God and His Divine principles personally and professionally as she walks out His vision for her life. A woman of wisdom who has shared her knowledge and the lessons that she has learned with others to help pave the way. A woman of compassion who has been a welcoming space for countless people in need of a listening ear, a kind word, and a gentle heart. Cissy has shown herself to be of excellent character as she continues to build a strong legacy for her family that will last for generations. She is an empowering mother who has modeled and instilled qualities of excellence in her children who will help to change the world.

Cissy's journey to becoming The Millionaire Woman has been marked by trials and triumph. Despair and joy. Challenge and achievement. She has endured circumstances and situations that would have waylaid anyone else. God has transformed her adversities into steppingstones that have helped move her through every obstacle. He has been with her through every instance of breakthrough and kept her feet upon the path.

I have watched this extraordinary woman as she has lived her life fully and with as much love and courage as she has to offer. I have been encouraged as she has overcome divorce and failed relationships, family issues, financial issues, contract losses, and dishonorable people. I have also been inspired as I have watched her pain transform into healing through one of the most devastating experiences a person could face—the loss of her dear mother.

Despite these situations, and so many more, Cissy Watkins has been humble and open and always willing to learn. Despite the pain of whatever challenges she has faced, she has stayed consistent in activating her faith and never losing her zest, enjoyment, and gratitude for the life that God has given her.

This is what truly makes her The Millionaire Woman.

Congratulations, Beloved Ones. You have picked up a book about a woman whose desire to share with you can inspire you to another level of living.

Blessings to you always!

-Jai Staton

Introduction

Why haven't you made it to the shining beacon of a successful business that is a marker of accomplishment for you? The successful business that can be the cornerstone of an incredibly fulfilling and productive life. You are closer than you've ever been. You've worked harder, learned from your mistakes, recovered from challenges, celebrated triumphs, and leaned into trusting God more with your whole heart. You are so close. But it still seems to elude you, for one reason or another. This book is going to help you discover and correct the reason(s) that you do not have the successful business you are working so hard to build. Does it have all the answers? No. Does it have enough information to help you get to all the answers? Yes, it does.

Your journey to a million has already begun. If you are ready to continue the journey because you believe you and the life you desire are worth it, keep reading. This book offers solutions, encouragement, and the support you need for your successful business journey. Prepare to embrace this next part of your path as I provide you with more tools to prosper and position you for good success.

CHAPTER 1

Who Not To Hire

"Who Hired Who? To Do What?"

In my desire to be a contributor to my family, friends, and community, I overlooked one crucial aspect to building a successful business—making good hires.

For small business owners, the recruiting and retention of good employees is a top challenge. This first lesson can help you to overcome major mistakes in this area.

The Lesson

If you decide to hire people that you know, make sure you have the hard and necessary conversations with them first. Be open and honest and set proper expectations. Know who not to hire—and why.

The Experience

I cannot tell you all the stories that I have endured in learning this lesson. I have repeated it several times over because I did not practice some of the things that I learned. I have had people I know bring their children onto a restricted work site. I have caught referred hires in compromising situations. I have been fined because of family and family-related hires; that means I lost money. I have given business authority to friends, family, and church members and found out later they did not have the skill sets or work ethic needed to be an employee with my company, let alone to be a trusted decision maker. It really turned out that for the most part, my family, friends, and church members were not on the same level that I was on business wise. People that you know, that you choose to hire, HAVE TO BE on a certain level or it is not going to work out. When I say a certain level, I am referring to the mindset that you want your employees to have. One of the best ways to ensure your mindset and expectations are in alignment is by having a conversation. A conversation is required to set clear expectations. It is also enlightening as you go through your hiring process. Not only should you be looking to see if the candidate is a good fit for your company, the candidate should be asking some of the same questions of you as well.

The experiences I had were hurtful, and I had to come to understand that ATL&C Cleaning Service was MY Vision. Even though I wanted to create a legacy for my family, and I know that was a noble reason, that did not automatically put everyone on the same level of understanding and commitment as me. You should know that same truth about your business. Anyone you hire to represent YOUR COMPANY and YOUR VISION must have a certain mindset, and you should think carefully about what qualities you want your employees to have. And after your thinking is done, you must follow up with the right actions to help support your vision.

I also want to emphasize the importance of being honest with yourself here. Everyone knows that Cousin Bobby has never been able to hold down a job. There is a reason for that. And now he wants to come work for you. You have to be ready to have that conversation and make the decisions that come with it.

As a servant of God, who loves to serve people, I could not hire every person who seemed friendly or Godly or even had a good resume. I learned how to seek out the qualities that people had in addition to the skill sets that I desired for the position. This is a very important and sometimes overlooked part of the hiring process.

Consider your job descriptions and how you process candidates carefully. Use whatever tools you have available to discern or discover whether someone has the characteristics and qualities you value in addition to the skills needed to be successful.

Hiring and employee turnover are some of the biggest costs with running your business. It is crucial that you find several measures of successful operations in this area.

Also, as a servant of God and a woman of integrity, I never ask anyone to do anything for free. It is a blessing and an honor to be able to provide people in my community with good jobs. I take this responsibility very seriously. I must make good decisions to continue moving my vision forward. You will need to do the same.

We also must be very realistic about some of the other pitfalls of the hiring process. Hiring out of desperation, unknown hiring bias, failure to use all the resources possible to evaluate a candidate, and not being prepared to fully interview an applicant are all problems that usually lead to bad hires. You can avoid all of these, for the most part, and find ways to operate that fully support you and your vision. And you can find the people who will do this also.

The Why

Another reason that you should steer clear of hiring your family, friends, and church members is because sometimes they will feel entitled because they know you personally. And sometimes, okay, a lot of times, they will try to use it to their advantage. They want to be paid, but they may feel like and act like they do not have to give you 100 percent. However, they expect to be paid the same, and more sometimes, than other employees. You will never get the same 100 percent commitment and work ethic out of people you know personally as you would get out of people you do not know. And please keep in mind that this has been MY experience. I really did not want to use the word 'entitlement' here. It's been thrown around and overused a lot, especially in the social climate in which we currently find ourselves. But it is true and accurate. Because family, friends, and church members know you on a personal level, the temptation to abuse the relationship is present at all times and takes a really strong and focused mindset to overcome any illusion of entitlement because they "know the boss". We all know people like this. How do you feel about them?

This Really Happened

A family member who was working for me was a no-call, no-show for a shift. When I contacted the employee (note, when I contacted him) to find out about his absence, he replied with, "Well, you knew it was my birthday, so you should have known that I was not coming in to work." Yes. That really happened.

Listen

If God gave you a vision, He will send you who you need to manifest the vision. And those people will be able to fill in the places where you are weak and make your vision, and your business, stronger.

The Scripture

II Cor. 4:17 AMP

"For our momentary, light distress [this passing trouble] is producing for us an eternal weight of glory [a fullness] beyond all measure [surpassing all comparisons, a transcendent splendor and an endless blessedness]!"

Yes, you will deal with challenging situations; and yes, you will have to make decisions that some may not agree with or understand. In the end, God is always in control. And He will take your vision and your business to where it needs to be regardless of challenges.

Mantra/Affirmation

I will not hire anyone without first consulting with my HR team or a trusted professional or business partner.

Action Steps

- Try to avoid hiring family, friends, or church members without proper screening and supportive systems in place.
- Define what a "good hire" or "good candidate" looks like to you. Let this knowledge guide you in your decisions regarding who you hire and who you don't.
- Consult with an HR Professional regarding your hiring decisions.
- This may mean you secure a professional for a one-time consulting conversation or you locate a

professional so you can completely outsource this task, or any other options you can strategically design. The goal here is to remember the lesson and have a plan in place so you don't have to endure it and, as I did, repeat it.

CHAPTER 2

Minding Your Own Business

"That is Not My Business"

How hard could it be to do my own accounting and bookkeeping? It cannot be that hard. I have been managing my household, my hobbies, and business finances for years. If this is your line of thought, I have five words especially for you:

No. Do not do this.

As a matter of fact, do not do anything that you do not already have a high level of mastery in.

The Lesson

Never do your own books. No bookkeeping or accounting for you. No. Never. Just do not do it. Mind your OWN Business and pay someone to do these for you. As the cool kids say, "Stay in your lane." (Do they still say that? Moving on.) There is also an assorted number of professionals you may need to help you get your business established like a well-run, efficient, money-making machine. This could be a marketing person, an IT person, HR, someone to create/manage website, etc. So keep in mind—minding your business means you are making decisions to support your business in the best possible ways. That can mean you hire other competent and experienced professionals to do it for you.

The Experience

Some business owners will tell you that if you do not have an IRS story, you have not been in business long enough. I am here to tell you that that may be true, but it does not have to be that way for you.

Let me tell you my little IRS story. Actually, there's two of them. (smile)

I was sitting at home one day, enjoying the fact that things were running smoothly with my business and that

I could kick back and redeem a little down time. A knock at the door interrupted me and when I opened it, it was the IRS. At my house. Not at my business office. AT MY HOUSE. Asking to come in and speak with me. Jesus.

They came in, sat down, and proceeded to tell me there were some problems regarding my taxes that were really years in the making. Years of me working to keep up with my accounting and bookkeeping, in addition to all the other hats that I attempted to wear on a regular basis. They asked for my bank statements, which I provided, and they began to go down a list and cross off everything on my bank statement. I was not sure what they were doing as they went over my bank statements. Were they trying to find the errors? Were they looking for more problems? No, none of that. They were looking at what and who I paid monthly. And then they told me the things I could no longer pay so that I could pay them and get my tax situation corrected. They crossed off everything I could no longer pay—including my tithes. When the IRS tells you what you can and cannot do with your own hard-earned money, you better learn the lesson that is required.

Never do your own books. Get a professional bookkeeper or CPA.

Now, do not get me wrong. This was a positive interaction for the most part. Besides the fact that I had screwed some things up and it was costing me money, the IRS agents were very nice.

On another occasion, I went into the IRS office because I discovered I was behind on my taxes due to being overworked and overwhelmed, and not really minding my own business. I was still working a full-time job and needs were growing, professionally and personally. I wanted to get everything straightened out before "The People" came knocking at my door—again. In this instance, they were holding up checks from my biggest contractor at the time. I had several thousand dollars simply in limbo. And not in my bank account. To make a long story super short, God placed a lady from the IRS before me who was a sister in The Kingdom and obedient to His Voice. She reviewed my case and simply said, "Release her money." Thank you, God, for Ms. Patricia and always putting people in places to help us move Your Vision and Your Kingdom forward.

The Why

You do not know everything. And you do not need to. You need other people who can guide you in areas you do not know about. Other people who may have the right knowledge for your situation. I understand the things you have to think about to make your business go and grow daily. I truly do. But please, please know that you need to make sure you "Mind Your Own Business". Your accounting, bookkeeping, back office functions, and other various services are important because not only do you pay yourself and take care of your family, you have others that you pay also. There has been one time, in 15 years, I had to tell my employees they would not be paid on time. And it was because I was not minding my business. When people trust you to the point they know you will take care of them, despite challenges, it is an honor and a privilege that I know God allowed me to have. I am blessed to have been able to navigate around and through these challenges as they have arrived. And I am also blessed to be able to say I have learned from every mistake I have made, even if some of them were on repeat. And I am so grateful for all my experiences because now I get to share them with you. Amen.

Listen

Get a knowledgeable team of professionals around you who can support your vision, share good information with you, and most importantly, help your business stay healthy and well. A money team that can appropriately address and take care of the financial well-being of your company. Remember when I said I was overwhelmed and overworked? That state of mind greatly influenced how

I made decisions about minding my business. I loved my trusted CPA and his family dearly. But as my business grew, so did the financial needs of my business. His business was growing as well. I discovered that I didn't just need a CPA. I needed a bookkeeper. I needed a wealth manager. I needed an insurance expert. I needed a tax attorney. So many things that required so many different areas of knowledge. And I learned that I had to get these professionals in order to do business well. During this time, I was not effectively Minding My Business. I had to get a team to help me do it.

Keep in mind that this chapter doesn't just apply to the professionals I am mentioning here. Only you can discern what the most pressing needs are for your business. My encouragement is that you think critically about what you need and then go forward to get it. My tax stories were critical lessons and still hold a special place in my journey. Whatever the needs are for your business, as it grows and as you manage its growth, do an honest analysis to determine what professionals you need to help support you.

And also, when you are looking for professionals to support your business, get a consultation, ask questions that are pertinent to your business, and get referrals. When I say ask questions, I mean ask the hard questions. How often do you miss deadlines? Do you have a contingency plan if you are unable to complete expected work by deadlines? How do you back up your work? What if I am not satisfied with your level of service? Do not just take someone's word that they can do what you are requesting. Sometimes, many times, there is a lot more involved than just the job title and a skill set or two. Remember, you are going to be paying them for a service that is valuable to your efficient business operations. Which in turn means it can affect your income. This can be either a positive or negative effect. You want it to be positive.

The Scripture

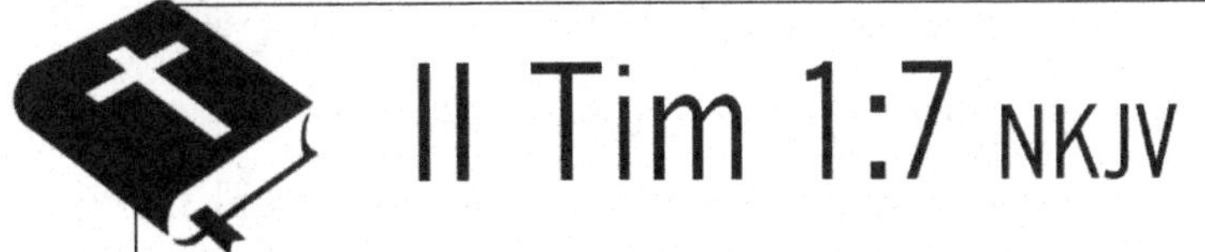

Use these gifts, especially that sound mind. All The Time.

Mantra/Affirmation

I will hire professionals to support and protect my business and my assets. This helps to create a stronger legacy for my children in every way. I will make sure to ask the right questions based on the needs of my business and what I desire to achieve.

Action Steps

- You should honestly evaluate your business and determine where and what you need to outsource to get the support and expertise your business requires. If you need other professionals, create a plan to source them, find them, and contract with them.
- Make strategic decisions about contracting other professionals and ask them questions that are crucial to the infrastructure and foundation of your business. You should also make sure to talk to them about the growth plans of your business.
- My strongest suggestion to you? Get yourself a money team—a CPA, a bookkeeper, a financial advisor, an insurance agent, and a broker. Everyone has a specialty that they master and they all contribute to making sure that my finances, and my knowledge of them, grows.

CHAPTER 3

No Compromise

"Put God first in Your Business"

As a Christian Business Owner, the only way to run your business is to make sure you reflect the principles of the Kingdom of God in all you do. Even, and especially, when you are dealing with people who may not share your beliefs or values. Let me be very clear here—compromise is not a bad thing. But it can be if you are not careful.

The Lesson

When people—employees, potential employees, family members, friends, customers, potential clients, or anyone—ask you to compromise your business principles or your values, say no and move on. Let your no be NO. Never compromise your values or your business principles. Not to make a dollar. Not to get along or go along. Not because you do not want to offend anyone. Do not compromise on your values or your business principles. Put God first. ALWAYS. Remember your purpose and your vision.

When I decided to partner with God and base all my decisions on His principles, my business took off and went to new levels. And it allowed me to be able to discern whether or not a situation was the right one for me.

The Experience

When you are confronted with people who ask you, either directly or indirectly, to compromise on your values and the principles that you have built your business on, you have a choice to make. I have had people ask me to give them a job but say they need to be paid "under the table" or "off the books". No, I am unable to do that. Move On. I have had people who do not have legal work authorization documents attempt to work for me stating they have not had problems with their identification numbers before, knowing that the numbers they gave my HR team were not legitimate. And just as a side note, these people expected to work for me and did not see anything wrong with asking me to risk my business. That is what they were doing, regardless of whether they realized it or not. Asking me to risk my business.

There have been countless experiences over the years in which I have had to take a deep breath and think with clarity about my next decisions and steps. Is this the right thing to do? Is this the right thing to do now? Some answers will be very clear, others you may need to consider for a bit. The blessing is that God is always with you and His guidance is always readily available for you. Don't take His grace for granted.

The Why

People asking you to compromise your business principles and your values do so thinking it is not a big deal and their small request is not going to have an impact on your business. And honestly, most of the time, they do not care that it can have an impact on your business. They are just trying to get what they feel they need. But this is where they are wrong. And you will be too if you make an incorrect choice. It is a beautiful and blessed thing to be able to help others, but helping others without thinking about how your decisions can impact your business is a mistake. Additionally, making any choices without consulting The Creator can have unintended consequences. The blessing here is that God promises He will work all things out for our good. And He does. But we do not have to make things harder for ourselves by making choices that do not put God first in our lives and our businesses.

Making decisions that compromise your values to appease others will only result in challenges that you will have to reap the consequences for, alone. The person that asked you to pay them under the table? They found another job after your payroll is screwed and you are trying to justify a payroll expense that is not a payroll expense to the IRS. The person who did not present a valid social security number for work authorization? That one violation can cost anywhere from $548-$4384. One violation. An employer can also face criminal and civil penalties. And not with the IRS, but with ICE—U.S. Immigration and Customs Enforcement. The potential client that asked you to conduct your business in dishonorable ways to help them get an advantage? They have moved on to trying to get another entrepreneur to agree to some get rich money scheme. And because they do not have a legal business, they are not feeling compromised in any way. But you and your legit business could be.

Listen

Always think strategically about building a reputable, honorable, and sustainable business for The Kingdom and for yourself and your family. If one of your goals is to create a legacy for your family, then there is only one way to do business. That is by operating with and on God's principles. Do not let anyone sway you to compromise your values or your principles because they are trying to get what they feel they need. Their need is not your issue and their challenge is not yours. You run a business. A successful Kingdom based business. You do not run a volunteer service. You do not run a non-profit. (Well, maybe you do, but that will be covered in another book.) You do not run an "under the table" operation. Do not act like you do by making a compromise that can impact everything in a negative way.

The Scripture

If you have been called to the marketplace to do Kingdom business, then do business the Kingdom way.

Mantra/Affirmation

I will not compromise my values or principles. I will always put God first.

Action Steps

- Think back over any times when you have been asked to make a compromise regarding your business.
- What decisions did you make, and were they the right ones? As you think about these things, resolve to either make better decisions going forward or to continue building good decision making that does not compromise your business in any way.
- If building a successful legacy based on The Kingdom model is your goal, then the path will be made available for you.

CHAPTER 4

Crossing Boundaries

"Don't"

Setting and enforcing proper boundaries eliminates risk for your company and provides a clear framework for how you operate your business. When you know where you stand, it makes it infinitely easier to not cross boundaries.

The Lesson

Set proper boundaries with everyone. This means clients, customers, friends, and employees. Everyone.

Dictionary.com says that a boundary is "something that indicates bounds or limits". You need to know your limits or where you draw the line in how you deal with people and business. Setting and sustaining boundaries is essential to good business (and personal) development. It can give you a sense of agency and empowerment. But it also lets you know when you need to cut ties with people or sometimes, other businesses or entities.

Setting proper boundaries requires that you be aware of your guiding principles and values and that you honor those in word and deed. If you say you believe in doing business honestly, but you enter into a contract with someone who shows themselves to not be honest, then a boundary has been breached and you will need to take necessary action to sever the contract. That is just one of many examples in this lesson.

The Experience

Crossing boundaries for me has always been the result of me operating from my emotions and not with my business or spiritual sense.

Do not get emotionally attached to anyone, especially employees. Setting up and maintaining proper boundaries will help with this. When I found myself trying to do things to help people outside of boundaries that I should have set, it always ended up becoming a problem. Setting proper boundaries protects you from the attachments that can come from being too involved in another person's life or responsibilities. As a business owner and an employer, it is your duty to employ people in the community who support your vision. It is not your duty to make sure your employees can take care of their families or pay their bills. There is a difference.

I have had employees tell me about their personal health issues, car troubles, and family situations with the expectation that I will take responsibility for their issue.

"Ms. Cissy, I have six kids to feed."

"Yes, but that is not Ms. Cissy's responsibility. I need you to be at work on time as agreed. If you cannot make it to work on time for your shift daily, then we will have to make other arrangements. We made an agreement when you started working for me. That agreement does not change because you share your personal situation with me. I expect you to complete your obligation, just as you expect me to do with mine and pay you for your hours worked."

This is not to say that you should be callous or unfeeling towards your employees. It is to say that you should set yourself up to ensure that they understand where the boundaries are and how you apply them.

To be quite honest, you should find a way to deter employees from sharing too much of their personal life with you anyway. I care about my employees. But I had to be very careful and diligent about setting boundaries so that there is no confusion about my business values and the working agreement I may have with employees. Yes, an employee can share with you that they had a car issue on the way to work and that is why they are going to be late. It should stop there. And you can take a moment here to remind them of whatever your attendance policy is so that there is little to no room for misunderstanding what is expected and what you can allow. This sets a clear boundary for you and for them. I do know some managers and owners who will tell employees outright that they do not care about their reasons for being late or having absences. I understand why they do this, but I also recognize that there is a better way, again, a Kingdom way, to do business. I can set boundaries and let people know them without compromising their humanity in the process.

I know that in our society, we, especially African American women, have been socialized to think that we are supposed to sacrifice ourselves for others and that there is a level of nobility in self-sacrifice. Incorrect. Jesus paid it all and I will not sacrifice the legacy I am building for my family because you expect me to make a sacrifice for you and break clear boundaries that I have set for a reason. Look at Jesus for that. Not me and my business. I am not your ram in the bush.

"Ms. Cissy, I don't have gas money."

"Ms. Cissy, can you loan me thirty dollars?"

"Ms. Cissy, I know my schedule is Friday, Saturday, and Sunday, but I can't work weekends."

In all these instances, a conversation must be held in order to let the person know they are asking you to cross a boundary that is important to you and your business. And it is imperative that you let them know where you stand.

"Thank you for trusting me with your information. But I do not loan money to employees. I do hope that everything works out for you." That is a clear boundary. "If you are unable to work the schedule that you were offered and agreed to, then I have to find someone who can fulfill this agreement. You are released from duty. If anything comes available that will fit your schedule, I will call you."

I have said to people, "Call Mr. Wal-Mart and ask him to give you thirty dollars. See what he says and then get back to me. If you cannot or have not asked other employers for money, then why would you ask me?"

I remember one specific experience that still challenges me sometimes.

An employee asked me to give her an advance in August. She asked again in September. I told her, "Maybe you should find another job to supplement your income."

She said, 'Well, you know I can't because I have children." That is not my problem, challenge, or responsibility. Setting proper boundaries can keep employees from even sharing that kind of information with you. Again, it is not that I do not care about my employees or their families. But I am very clear on where my boundaries are and what I am not willing to do. Or not do. Sometimes these kinds of conversations can be a twofold attempt to make you feel guilty and responsible at the same time. Do not allow anyone to take your kindness and gracious spirit for their use. It will always come back to bite you.

The Why

When you do not set proper boundaries, it allows for a whole new set of expectations. And often, incorrect expectations. You, and your business, will be the ones that will ultimately suffer the consequences.

Not setting proper boundaries can also lead to several other unintended consequences. Allowing an employee to assume a level of comfort with you and you assuming a level of comfort with an employee blows the doors off boundaries and can make your business life harder than it has to be.

You do not want to ever become invested in the personal lives of your employees. You should never bear that burden as a boss or employer. It is one thing to build good relationships with your employees, but you are building good, professional relationships. That is another challenge in hiring family, friends, and church members. You may already know some of their business, and they may know some of yours. That does not mean they receive, nor should they expect, special treatment because of that relationship.

Another unintentional effect of not setting proper boundaries can be that you can keep people from their God moments. You must be able to allow people to experience God in their own ways and wanting to cross boundaries can keep them from an experience they may need. We all have been through difficult and sometimes downright awful challenges, but my hope is that you learn to always seek and trust God, even in those moments. Other people have to learn to do this as well, in whatever ways God has designed for them. We have to trust His Word and His leadings in this area.

Crossing boundaries can cause people to look at you as if you could be their way to get through things. You do not want to be that. Well, not in healthy relationships anyway.

Do not misunderstand the message in this chapter. We are called to serve the Kingdom of God, but we must use our discernment in order to stay aligned with God's vision for His Business. Your business is a way to build the Kingdom, a platform to help bring people closer to God.

I have had the blessings of having old employees call me to ask me to pray for them because of something they were going through. Past employees have called me to apologize and to share how my boundaries in their situation helped them to a breakthrough they did not know they needed.

Listen

Make sure you always work to set clear and solid boundaries for employees, customers, and clients as well. (We should also make sure to do this with family and friends, but that is a whole other book!) I want to see everybody win, but I had to set clear boundaries. When I did things my way, everybody was winning except me. I worked longer and harder and lost more money. I started winning when I remembered that my business was a Kingdom based business and that I had to do things the Kingdom way. Not only did I start winning, so did all the people that God aligned with me.

In the process, you must understand that people only do what you allow them to do. I cannot change who God created me to be. I am a woman who was built to serve others and I love it. But, I had to learn to create and enforce real boundaries in order to be an effective Kingdom entrepreneur. There is no need for me to be out here trying to do work that my good brother Jesus already did.

I live by the fact that My Show is Kingdom and my business is My Show. We lead with The Kingdom, we show examples, and we do everything in love. No matter if you do not receive it or like the answer. And that is why I'm a multi-millionaire.

The Scripture

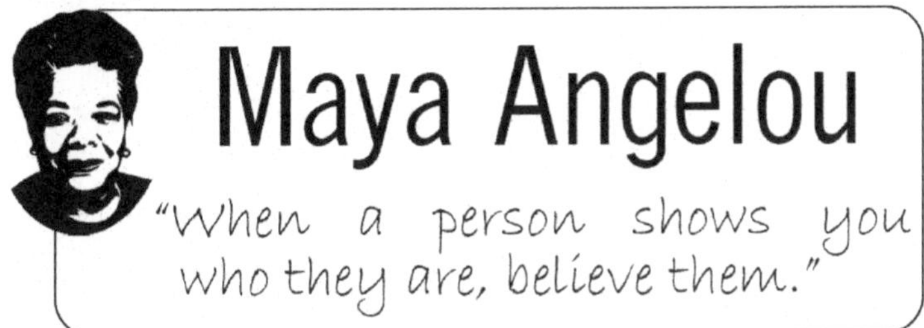

Okay, so this is not a scripture, but it is relevant to put into action here. It is gospel though. (wink and smile)

Mantra/Affirmation

I will set clear boundaries and I will be consistent and faithful with enforcing them.

Action Steps

Set up clear boundaries for everyone that you encounter and be consistent with enforcing those boundaries. These actions can create chaos or peace in your Kingdom business depending on which one you choose.

CHAPTER 5

The Black and White

"Sticking to Policies and Procedures"

You are running a successful business. There are a lot of things to consider, decide, and act on as a successful business owner. In this lesson, we will talk about why sticking to policies and procedures is crucial to the success of your business. I like to call it the black and white of your business.

The Lesson

Adhering to your defined standards of operations, policies, and procedures can make your business run smoother and be more effective. You also need to know that things change, that you change, that business needs change, and that adjusting is an essential part of growth. This does not mean that you disregard the core of your business policies and practices. Work diligently to keep your goals in mind in any situation.

Operating your business without a black and white area guarantees that you will be all over the place, in every area. This is similar to not crossing boundaries but differs a bit. Deciding what is most important in each aspect of your business, what your goals are, and a plan of how to get there, will keep you operating in the right ways and help you stay consistent and true to your brand and mission.

> *"Focus means saying no to the hundred other good ideas."*
> **-Steve Jobs**

Who really wants to say no to an opportunity to do more of what they love? I love cleaning. I know that I am great at it. But, I also know I have had to be specific about what I will and will not do in order to stay upright on my path. There are times that I have been offered extensive cleaning contracts, and after going into prayer and meditation with The Divine, have opted to turn down those contracts. I was able to understand that all money was not good money and put that phrase to its highest use.

The Experience

I had a personable employee who was a great worker with personal and family issues that he made well-known. I listened to pieces of his life story with each incident that occurred that had an impact—some small, some large—on my business. I kept him on despite knowing that he should be terminated; and keeping him on came back to bite me in a few different ways.

I am not in the business of saving people. And neither are you—I mean, unless you are in that profession. I forgot this important piece of information when the situation was clearly black and white in regard to this employee. My company had policies in place that clearly dictated what should be done in this situation. I steadfastly refused to follow those policies until I had received customer complaints (sadly, more than one) in regard to his performance. Of course, his work performance was compromised, he is not focused on meeting work standards because of his constant, challenging personal situations. Now I must explain to a customer who expects excellent service, why they are not receiving excellent service. A situation that I could have avoided entirely by adhering to the black and white policies of my business operations.

The Why

If an employee is not performing as expected and agreed, then a separation is required. Delaying that can have serious negative impacts on your brand. One of the last things you ever want is to get an email from an unhappy customer or client due to an employee situation that you knew about and could have acted to prevent. (I know I just said that, but I cannot overstate this point.) Delaying actions in cases like this can also cause relationships to not end in the best ways. Think about it; if you are used to providing a mediocre performance and then having a conversation with the boss in which you detail how challenging your life is and then you continue your job with very little consequences, how would you feel when you are terminated? Most employees do not view this situation with their actions top of mind. Instead, they may feel as if they have been wronged by the employer. If your mission is "operating in the spirit of excellence" (again, mine is!), it means you uphold that mission for internal and external customers. And for yourself. Adhering to your policies and procedures gives you the opportunity to be transparent and just when dealing with everyone. This is a big part of excellent service.

Determining and following the black and white of any situation can give you valuable insights into vendor and customer relations also. While it is always a given that "the customer is always right", we know there is some room for individual interpretation and insight in these situations. Use these insights, and the valued ones of colleagues, to make sure you are acting in accordance with your policies.

Listen

This can be a challenging part of business ownership, but do not turn away. Your brand, your impact, and so many other things depend on how well you manage the black and white so that you can stay out of the red and in the green.

The Scripture

James 1:25 ESV

But the one who looks into the perfect law, the law of liberty, and perseveres, being no hearer who forgets but a doer who acts, he will be blessed in his doing.

Set the law for your business and look to it for making sound, just decisions and actions.

Mantra/Affirmation

I commit to creating and following sound and righteous standards of operations, policies, and procedures that reflect good character, excellence, and The Kingdom.

Action Steps

- Take yourself out of the loop and hire someone to help you stick to your policies and procedures. This person can also be someone who helps you to revise policies as your business grows and changes.
- As a business owner, you can go as far as you like with your decision making. That does not mean you should.
- Identify your weaknesses, hire someone to cover that area, and then do not overstep the person who helps you to stay leveraged in that area.
- You have heard me say that before. Seeing the shift that began to happen in my business as I established and followed a supported and sensible standard of operations was a huge benefit. I want you to have some of those same benefits as well.

CHAPTER 6

Create

"Creativity and Problem-Solving Go Hand in Hand"

Sometimes solving a problem in your business means you need to fire up your creative juices before strapping on your sneakers and going to do it yourself. This can be a challenging and uncomfortable area for a lot of us because we are used to doing it ourselves. If you want something done, get others to do it. If you want something done right, do it yourself. Am I Right? No. Not always.

Get okay with being uncomfortable and thinking of new and different ways to accomplish your goals. Good solutions are always available to you. By that, I mean you are able to generate good solutions by using the talents God has given you—creativity is one of those talents.

The Lesson

The ability to be creative and think outside the box can bring big benefits and save you time and money in the process. Thinking through a problem and then coming up with creative ways to conquer the problem and reasonably ensure that it does not happen again are benchmarks for success. And it does not always mean some super radical change has to happen.

This can also mean that you may need to call on your network of resources in order to come up with viable solutions. This is a good thing. Sometimes the insight from others can be enough to ignite new ideas that can propel you through a difficult challenge. We do it all the time, even if we do not give ourselves enough credit for it.

What can this mean for your business? Let's talk about it.

The Experience

I needed a technician who could specifically clean and wax floors for a client. I hired a gentleman whom I had established contact with through a referral and thought him to be the person I needed for the job. We set up our contract and I began paying him. I checked in periodically to see how things were going and he assured me that things were fine. Then comes the email from the unhappy client with dirty floors. I reassured the client and spoke with my contractor who assured me that he would complete the job. Two months later and my client was still unsatisfied. Two months, dear readers.

A trusted partner, Leftie, said to me, “Get that client happy. Find someone who can make them happy.” Their floors were still not clean so yes, they were not happy. It was not their issue that I had hired someone to do it who did not complete the job, that was my responsibility. I was blessed that the client did not terminate my contract at that point. But guess whose contract was terminated? The guy who was supposed to do the floors. My first thought was to go get a floor machine and do the floor work myself—I had done it before. I calculated what it would take for me to get the job completed in a timely manner, even though it was already behind schedule. Time and energy that I did not have at that moment. It was in this place that I learned a few important things. I added key, dependable staff to keep me from having to “go do”. And I held them to a level of accountability that I had not previously enforced. All this was done after connecting with trusted support and coming up with solutions to the issue at hand.

The solution to the floor issue helped me to create good solutions in other areas of my business as well.

I really liked thinking about creating a dependable team of key people who could be my trusted point people in any situation. People that could keep me from having to say, "If you want something done right, you have to do it yourself." I didn't want to always be forced to do that. I began to look for and work towards those types of solutions. I began to think of other ways to get to the goal of having those types of people on my team. And I began to find them in the most unexpected ways and places.

The Why

There were so many benefits to becoming a creative problem solver for my business. It made my business run smoother because I was not running around everywhere putting out fires and trying to fireproof everything by myself. My supervisors and management team had my back and had the best interests of my company and its mission at their core. It allowed me to be more transparent with them and offered up another chance for me to solicit The Creator to send me people who could help me. I was not really thinking in the complete terms of "team" at first. He started sending me loyal people to help. And then, after

15 years of running everything by myself, God sent me a partner to help me see things I could not see and build in ways I had not imagined from inside my box. Collaborating with others and using my discernment helped to fuel my creative juices in ways that had great impacts on the way I conducted business.

Reaching towards new thoughts and ideas helped to spur my business forward and it helped to expand my faith in the strength of possibilities. It took courage for me to first admit I needed to find some new ways of doing things. Then it took commitment to intentional action to start moving my business forward. I even discovered that doing better with my self-care routine stimulated and supported my creativity and problem-solving skills. Believe me when I say that I am disciplined about using these lessons I have learned and that everything concerning me has been better because of it.

Listen

An apostle I know said that most people do not have money problems, relationship problems, or business problems—most people just have creativity problems. Pray and meditate on this when you encounter challenges. Ask God to show you where you are lacking and to help you remain open to solutions. Once God provides the guidance you need, and He will, it will be up to you to make the actions that can catapult your business to greater success.

The Scripture

...and He has filled him with the Spirit of God, with wisdom, with understanding, with knowledge and with all kinds of skills...

God tells us right here that He has given us everything we need. Be aware of the gifts and talents you have and work to master them. Even the ones you do not see as strengths. Use the resources that He has put at your disposal to keep moving forward.

Mantra/Affirmation

I will find and rediscover ways to help me retain my creativity and problem-solving abilities. I will do this by staying connected and listening for God's direction in all that I do.

Action Steps

- Pray first. Whatever the problem is, pray about it first and listen for God's response. He always responds.
- Never react emotionally or impulsively and never take things personally.
- Always move with the expectation of excellence, not ego.
- When dealing with an employee or contractor, always tag in HR, trusted support staff, or partners to help resolve situations.
- Always engage in proper self-care and take time away so you can be refreshed and creative.

CHAPTER 7

Is It a Business or a Hobby?

"Do You Know the Difference?"

People talk all the time about how they turned their hobby, side hustle, or passion into a business. It sounds great and implies that if you have any of those, you can turn them into a profitable, successful business. That is true, but there is a whole lot more to this business ownership world that can overwhelm you if you are not aware and prepared. Come walk and read with me, Beloved.

The Lesson

I have been running my business for 15 years. I did not know that I had a business until year seven. To borrow a millennial catch phrase, "How Sway?" Let me tell you.

When I started this journey, there were two things I knew. Two things. One was I wanted to create a legacy for my children. And two was I was passionate about cleaning—and very, very good at it.

The Experience

Here is the difference between a hobby and a business. A hobby is something you love to do and in which you expect to gain enjoyment but have no financial expectations (usually). A business is a service you perform for the public with financial expectations (garnering a profit while providing a service). This is part of the reason why it took me so long to understand that I was indeed running a business.

I love to clean. As I stated, I am passionate about it really. And I always have been. When I was working a full-time job, taking care of my family, and trying to come up with ideas to help move us closer towards our goals, I was not thinking about what business I could start. My idea was, "I love to clean." How could I create a life to do more of that than working in the corporate business environment? Do not misunderstand, I had a decent job and was well-liked by my colleagues, but I was searching for something more, even though I did not fully understand that at the time. So, I started cleaning a business or two after hours. It was surreal that my passion and commitment for cleaning kept growing and growing and eventually replaced my full-time job and became the sole provision for my family. I was making money, but I did not go into it with the idea that I was going to start and run a successful business. I did not go to any business start-up seminars. I did not create a point by point business plan. I did not even create a to-do list. I just talked to a few people, made some agreements, bought some mops, and got started. (Okay, there was a little bit more involved in it than that, but you get it. Right?)

I wanted to create a legacy for my children and generations to come. Of course I did. Did I think that cleaning up someone's offices would do that for my family? Not at all, but it did, and I am looking straight up at God as I always have.

In year seven, that's right, seven, I looked up and said, "Okay God, what are we doing? It seems like I have a business, but I'm operating like it's a hobby." I realized that if the cleaning thing kept climbing, I was going to have to make some decisions and actions. My next moves, based on God's answers, changed everything for me and my family.

I revamped my whole business structure and created a business plan. (Again Beloveds, year seven. I also revamped myself in the process!) I began to understand that the financial portion was the biggest piece to learn, and I began to seek out people who could help me learn about all the areas of entrepreneurship. I sought out people who were working in fields that I needed help in—finances, accounting, human resources, management, and personal and business mentors. I began to connect with folks who had avenues of knowledge that I needed and that I could support in their endeavors as well. I learned how to establish and maintain productive business relationships and to align all things with my mission of "Operating in the Spirit of Excellence."

The Why

Clearly defining whether or not you have a business or a hobby will help determine how you create success for your venture. The level of commitment that is required for a business is wholly different than what is needed for a hobby, and you get to be the master of that designation. This is not to say that hobbies are not important or that they cannot be businesses. It is to say that the needs of a successful business are vastly different from those of a hobby and you get to determine how you move with each.

Making these kinds of decisions, and the actions that need to accompany them, are crucial to your business success.

Listen

For a lot of us, it may prove to be a daunting task—aligning your passion with your ability to create a sustainable income for your family. Keep in mind, you see people every day who have found a way to discover and live their passion and generate a great income from that—why not you? Again, there is no easy work, easy road, or overnight success on this journey. While there are folks who may make it seem like that is the case, it most certainly is not for most of us. Think of what you may have come to know about a celebrity or a famous artist. One song, one show, one play, at the right moment, can make them a household name and an "overnight success".

Never mind that they have been living in their car for three years or they were selling homemade underground mixtapes and CDs for five years before they "made it". Whatever it was they were passionate about came to the forefront and started making provision for them, their families, and others. Your level of commitment is everything.

The Scripture

Jeremiah 29:11 NIV

"For I know the plans I have for you," declares the Lord, "plans to prosper you and not to harm you, plans to give you hope and a future.

We can count on the promises of God. If He has plans to give us hope and a future, keep walking the path. He will do just what He has said.

Mantra/Affirmation

I will learn and trust the purpose that God placed in me and I will honor Him in all that I do.

Action Steps

- Do an honest review of your business or hobby. Ask trusted colleagues/partners to help you evaluate, if needed.
- Are you really running a business that looks like a hobby? Are you really enjoying a hobby saying it's

a business? Be honest so you can do the work that needs to happen next.

- Seek guidance, if needed, to take the next realistic and logical steps for your passion or venture.

CHAPTER 8

The Breakthrough(s)

When I think about the times that God has created incredible and unexpected breakthroughs for me in my professional and personal life, I am overjoyed at how much He has taken care of me and my family. There are always blessings when you trust God to move you along your path, His path. Breakthroughs are always answered prayers. Sometimes they are even answers to prayers you did not even realize you asked, but God hears our hearts in every situation.

I wanted to share a few of my breakthroughs with you. These are some things I would like for you to know that can help to encourage you on the journey.

- For me to become The Millionaire Woman, I've had to partner with God and allow Him to lead.
- I recognized that there were so many takers and not so many people who were pouring into me. It was hurtful, but a necessary lesson.
- I learned to keep core people close and to trust God with my relationships.
- I learned to allow God to move through me and my business. Sometimes I had to shut the world out and discern things from a spiritual perspective. He showed me how to make one million a year and maintain steadily at half a million a year, despite losing contracts.
- Do not chase money, let money chase you. This is a winning strategy.
- Always operate in the spirit of excellence.

Please know that I have had to demonstrate the lessons I learned. You will have to do the same.

- I hired people that I did not know.
- I asked the hard questions when deciding on how to use my resources wisely.
- I attended seminars and expanded my knowledge base as much as I could.
- I learned to listen to the Holy Spirit, even in business. I started ATL&C Cleaning Service alone and it seemed like everyone had a motive to want to work with me or for me. God sent people who have turned out to be a part of my long-term vision.

Keeping your faith strong is essential to your success as an entrepreneur. I have found many ways of doing that and they have become tools for me on the journey.

- I spend a lot of time in The Word—listening, studying, reading, and praying. I strive to keep The Word in my head, in my heart, and in my spirit. This helps me to know that I have enough strength, focus, and faith to understand and appreciate that God is my Source for everything.
- When I am traveling, I am not always listening to music. I may be listening to Audible, one of my favorite apps. Or I may be checking out a new podcast. I try to expose myself to new information and insights as much as possible. (My son says I have been in school since he was born—I'm a Lifelong Learner!)

- Even as I have dealt with the very human feelings of emptiness and loneliness that show themselves from time to time, I still seek God.
- I have also come to a solid understanding of the self-discipline that is required to be able to continue to move forward with success.

CHAPTER 9

The Bonus

I cannot tell you how grateful I am that you have given me the opportunity to share some of my experiences with you. I hope this book helps you gain abundance in every area of your personal and business life going forward.

As a thank you, I have included this Bonus Content and Free Gift for you.

Emotional Operations

Some studies have concluded that we make up to 90 percent of our decisions based on our emotions. This is something that you need to be aware of as a business owner so that you can leverage tools to help you maintain a good balance when you have to make decisions. Emotional decision-making can lead to so many consequences and sometimes, let's be honest, it is quite avoidable. Logical thinking can be a much more sound way to make valid decisions, but we don't always choose that first. I have been in so many situations where I have made decisions based on emotions and I have had to fix mistakes—some small, some large—later. I have also been in situations where my emotions have given me clues that things are off. The real lesson here is to make sure that when you are making decisions, you are in the best state of balance that you can achieve at the time. And to submit whatever it is to God. Yes, I know that things move fast, a lot, but I also know and believe that you sometimes have to make a choice in how you manage a matter and how quickly you do or do not respond.

Creating the Path

The path that I have walked in this journey has not been easy, but I am still grateful. It has not been filled with well-wishers and a multitude of supporters who uplift me at every turn. There are no parade routes for successful entrepreneurs—well, for most of us. As a fortunate and blessed business woman, I have had to create the path as I am traveling it—and that is something that you will not hear in a lot of business classes, seminars, and workshops. People will tell you about someone being a "trailblazer" or that they are "self-made", but you will find these terms are inaccurate for the most part. I am indeed grateful for all the people who have supported me, my family, and my business over the years. But this path was still one that I had to learn to walk with God. And that His path was the one that created The Millionaire Woman.

Your Free Gift
Business Start-Up Toolkit

Business Start Up Checklist

- O Decide on the name of the business or organization.
- O Determine DBA if needed and additional regulations.
- O Decide on status of entity—type of corporation or non-profit.
- O Register business with local authority—Clerk of Court, Register of Deeds, etc. (This will be location specific.)
- O Determine if you need to also register with your state in addition to local.
- O Obtain an EIN.
- O Create any needed Partnership Agreements—sign and notarize.
- O Business Licensing—this is not needed in some states. Also, some states only require registration or licensing at the local level. Understand the regulations for your state and adhere to them.
- O Open a business checking and a business savings account.
- O Create a viable Business Plan.
- O Start consulting with needed consultants— Branding, Marketing, Accounting, Social Media, Web Design, etc.
- O Hire any needed consultants.

- O Website Design—ask crucial questions.
- O Social Media Platform—research and coordinate strategies.
- O Create business cards, letterhead, marketing materials.
- O Design and develop your brand identity and strategy.
- O Develop Marketing Strategy.
- O Decide on launch events.
- O Create any need agreements—NDAs, etc.
- O Complete any needed additional paperwork or certifications—copyrights, trademarks, patents, etc.
- O Schedule meetings with any required consultants, team members, etc.
- O Obtain a Dunn and Bradstreet Number.
- O Set a date and open the doors to do business.

Made in USA - Kendallville, IN
1220471_9780578799605
01.04.2021 0807